I0879211

UPDOG

EXTREME SNOWBOARDING CHALLENGES

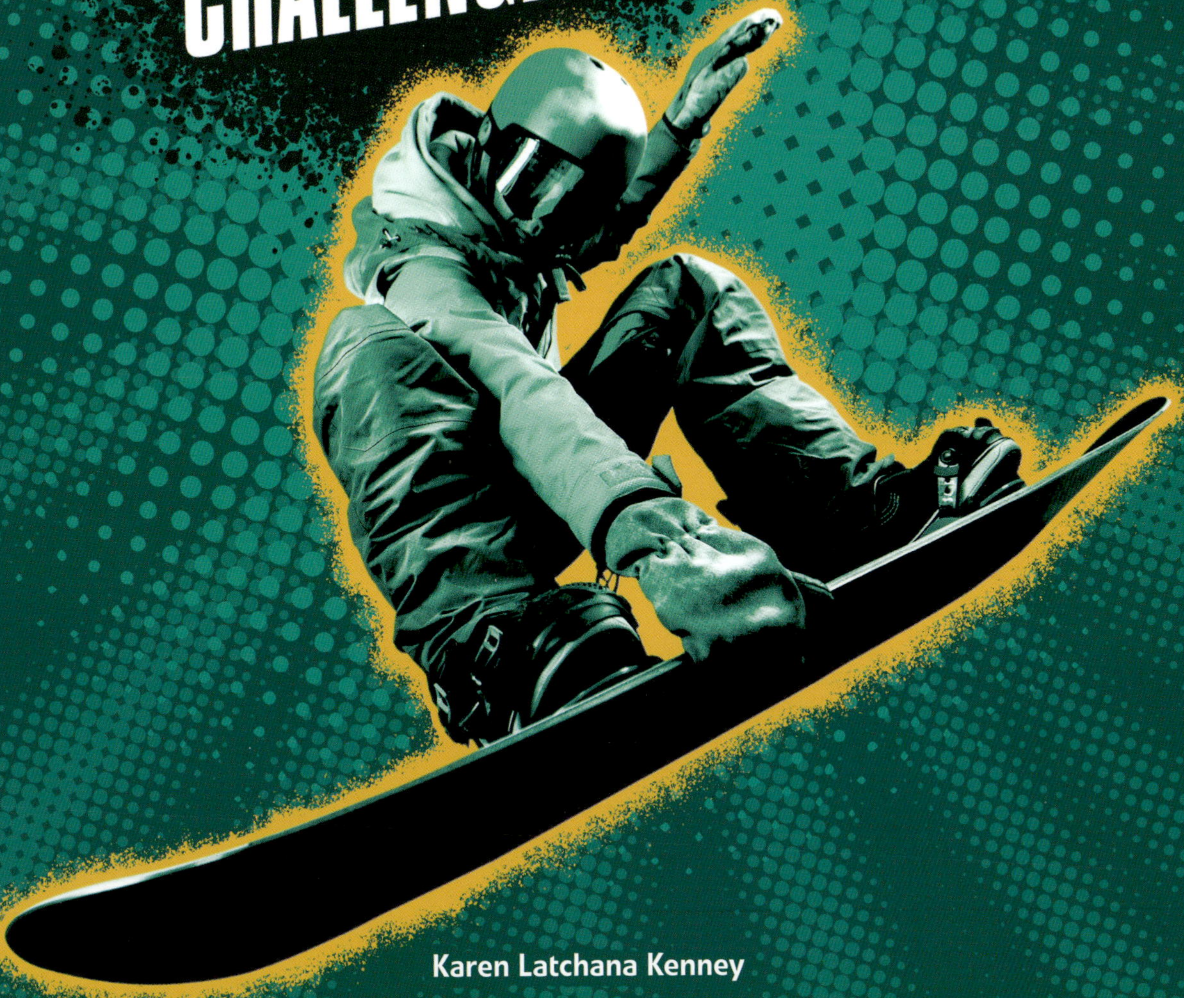

Karen Latchana Kenney

Lerner Publications ◆ Minneapolis

Copyright © 2021 by Lerner Publishing Group, Inc.

All rights reserved. International copyright secured. No part of this book may be reproduced, stored in a retrieval system, or transmitted in any form or by any means—electronic, mechanical, photocopying, recording, or otherwise—without the prior written permission of Lerner Publishing Group, Inc., except for the inclusion of brief quotations in an acknowledged review.

Lerner Publications Company
An imprint of Lerner Publishing Group, Inc.
241 First Avenue North
Minneapolis, MN 55401 USA

For reading levels and more information, look up this title at www.lernerbooks.com.

Main body text set in ITC Franklin Gothic Std.
Typeface provided by Adobe Systems.

Editor: Shee Yang **Designer:** Viet Chu
Lerner team: Sue Marquis

Library of Congress Cataloging-in-Publication Data

Names: Kenney, Karen Latchana, author. | Lerner Publishing Group, Inc.
Title: Extreme snowboarding challenges / Karen Latchana Kenney.
Description: Minneapolis : Lerner Publications, 2021. | Series: Extreme sports guides (UpDog Books) | Includes bibliographical references and index. | Audience: Ages 8–11 years | Audience: Grades K–1 | Summary: "Snowboarders blaze down a hill. They spin, flip, and dodge obstacles before crossing the finish line. Readers will learn all about snowboarding and how to train for an extreme contest!"— Provided by publisher.
Identifiers: LCCN 2020009480 (print) | LCCN 2020009481 (ebook) | ISBN 9781541590458 (Library Binding) | ISBN 9781728418155 (eBook)
Subjects: LCSH: Snowboarding—Juvenile literature. | Extreme sports—Juvenile literature.
Classification: LCC GV857.S57 K46 2021 (print) | LCC GV857.S57 (ebook) | DDC 796.939—dc23

LC record available at https://lccn.loc.gov/2020009480
LC ebook record available at https://lccn.loc.gov/2020009481

Manufactured in the United States of America
1-47564-48094-7/8/2020

Table of Contents

Boarding Big

Boarder Anna Gasser stood at the top of a 160-foot (48.8-m) ramp.

She launched into the air, flipped twice, and spun around three times.

ANNA GASSER

boarder: someone who snowboards

Gasser is an extreme slopestyle and big air snowboarder.

slopestyle: a snowboarding event on a course with obstacles

big air: a high jump in snowboarding and skateboarding

Boardercross and freeride are other types of snowboarding events.

boardercross: a snowboarding event where athletes follow a winding course with jumps

freeride: a snowboarding event on a natural mountain course

UP NEXT!

Training for the tricks.

Intense Training

Extreme snowboarders have strong legs.

They do squats, jumps, and lunges.

Balance training often includes BOSU balls.

BOSU ball: an inflated half ball often used for improving balance

Boarders stand on BOSU balls with one leg. They try not to fall off.

Bio Break!

Name: Shaun White

Age: 33

Hometown: San Diego, California

Claim to Fame:

- Three-time Olympic gold medalist for snowboarding
- Holds record for most X Games gold medals by a snowboarder
- Holds record for most Olympic gold medals by a snowboarder
- Has 10 Excellence in Sports Performance Yearly Awards

Snowboarding Hacks

- Learn how to fall. Falling correctly will prevent injury.
- Gear up and layer up. The right gear will keep you safe and warm!
- Protect your head. Wear a helmet.
- Keep dry. Prep your clothes with water repellent to help keep you dry.
- Learn more. Watch videos of snowboarders to understand their moves.

repellent: a substance that can be put on outerwear to help keep water from soaking in

Snowboarders also practice their tricks, such as ollies.

ollie: a snowboarding trick that makes the tip of a snowboard snap up

UP NEXT!

Extreme snowboarding competitions.

Extreme Competitions

The toughest snowboarders compete in extreme snowboarding competitions, like the Freeride World Tour.

From extreme speed to dangerous flips, competitors are judged on everything.

Snowboarding at the X Games is all about extreme tricks.

At the X Games, snowboarders have to be prepared for anything!

The Winter Olympics is the most extreme snowboarding competition.

Speed, technique, tricks, and landing are only some of the details that matter at the Olympics.

Glossary

big air: a high jump in snowboarding and skateboarding

boarder: someone who snowboards

boardercross: a snowboarding event where athletes follow a winding course with jumps

BOSU ball: an inflated half ball often used for improving balance

freeride: a snowboarding event on a natural mountain course

ollie: a snowboarding trick that makes the tip of a snowboard snap up

repellent: a substance that can be put on outerwear to help keep water from soaking in

slopestyle: a snowboarding event on a course with obstacles

Check It Out!

Adamson, Thomas K. *Big Air Snowboarding*. Minneapolis: Bellwether Media, 2016.

Ducksters: Snowboarding
https://www.ducksters.com/sports/extremesnowboarding.php

Kenney, Karen Latchana. *Extreme Skateboarding Challenges.* Minneapolis: Lerner Publications, 2021.

KidsHealth: Sledding, Skiing, Snowboarding, Skating
https://kidshealth.org/en/kids/winter-sports.html

PSIA-AASI: How to Snowboard
https://www.thesnowpros.org/take-a-lesson/beginners-guide-to-snowboarding

Schuh, Mari. *Snowboarding*. Mankato, MN: Amicus Ink, 2020.

Index

Photo Acknowledgments

Image credits: David Ramos/Getty Images, p. 4; Kyodo News Stills/Getty Images, p. 5; Kuznetsov Alexey/Shutterstock.com, p. 6; sportpoint/Shutterstock.com, p. 7; Syda Productions/Shutterstock.com, p. 8; Artem Varnitsin/Shutterstock.com, p. 9; Srdjan Randjelovic/Shutterstock.com, p. 10; lunamarina/Shutterstock.com, p. 11; Mahala Gaylord/The Denver Post/Getty Images, p. 12; ROBYN BECK/AFP/Getty Images, p. 13; Dmitry Molchanov/Shutterstock.com, p. 15; JOE KLAMAR/AFP/Getty Images, p. 16; JOE KLAMAR Getty Images, p. 17; Doug Pensinger/Getty Images, pp. 18, 19; Daniel Milchev/Getty Images, pp. 20, 21.

Cover: Artur Didyk/Shutterstock.com; rogistok/Shutterstock.com.